I0152809

Intuition: The Best Friend You Didn't Know You Had

Kelly Logan

Published by Better By Intent Publishing, 2025.

While every precaution has been taken in the preparation of this book, the publisher assumes no responsibility for errors or omissions, or for damages resulting from the use of the information contained herein.

INTUITION: THE BEST FRIEND YOU DIDN'T KNOW YOU HAD

First edition. December 2, 2025.

ISBN: 978-1971255026

Written by Kelly Logan.

Table of Contents

INTRODUCTION – You're Not Broken, You're Unaware

YOU'RE NOT FALLING behind.

You're not lacking anything.

You're not flawed, fragile, or missing some essential piece other people were mysteriously given.

You're simply unaware of what's already in you.

No one showed you how to trust your own inner signals. No one taught you how to listen inward or recognize the quiet steadiness that lives beneath all the noise. You didn't grow up hearing that clarity is natural, that intuition is built into you, or that peace is something you're supposed to feel from the inside out. Instead, you learned how to perform, how to endure, how to adjust yourself to the expectations around you.

You learned how to get through life, not how to belong to yourself within it.

This book isn't here to repair you.

It's here to reveal you.

Because underneath everything you picked up along the way—under the beliefs you absorbed without question, under the habits you repeated without noticing, under the versions of yourself you created to survive—there is a you who is calm, perceptive, grounded, and already whole.

Not eventually.

Not after you "fix" your life.

Right now, under the layers you've carried.

This is the version of you we're uncovering.

This is where your return begins.

Welcome back.

CHAPTER 1 – The World You Inherited

———

You didn't arrive on this planet unsure of yourself. You came in clear, steady, and naturally connected to an inner sense of direction that needed no explaining. But clarity doesn't survive untouched when you're born into a world full of people who lost theirs long before you showed up. You entered an environment where almost everyone was running on half-charged emotional batteries, doing the best they could with what they had, and unintentionally teaching you to live disconnected from yourself.

No one sat you down and said that there was a part of you that already knew what was right for you. Instead, you learned rules that had nothing to do with who you were: be easy, be pleasant, keep the peace, don't make waves, don't question adults, don't feel too loudly, don't want too much. You learned to shrink your awareness so it fit inside the emotional space other people could handle. You learned to look outward for direction because no one taught you that you already had an internal one.

Nothing about this was intentional harm. It was the world repeating its own survival code, passing down old strategies from one generation to the next without pausing to ask whether those strategies helped anyone. You absorbed the emotional atmosphere around you long before you understood what emotion even meant. Your nervous system adapted to whatever room you were in because that is how children stay safe: they adjust first and understand later.

That adaptation had a cost. Without realizing it, you built an identity out of pieces that didn't belong to you. You mirrored what you saw, assuming that was what life required. You learned to sense tension before it erupted, to soften yourself to avoid conflict, to quiet your reactions so you wouldn't be labeled as too much. You shaped yourself around the moods and expectations of others before you ever had the chance to discover your own.

You weren't taught self-trust; you were taught self-monitoring. You weren't taught to honor your internal signals; you were taught to override them. You weren't taught to listen inward; you were taught to scan the room. You weren't taught to check how things felt; you were taught to anticipate how things would look.

But here is the truth: you weren't broken then, and you're not broken now. You were surviving the environment you landed in. The world you inherited wasn't designed to nurture inner peace, intuition, or authenticity. It was designed to keep things functional on the surface, even if it meant disconnecting from what was real underneath. So you became what was required, believing that being agreeable or staying quiet was the price of safety.

Over time, you may have chased things that were supposed to make you feel whole—approval, relationships, accomplishments, belonging—only to discover they couldn't touch the emptiness inside. Not because you failed, but because those things were never meant to replace the connection you were missing with yourself. The world taught you how to perform a life but never taught you how to feel at home in one.

You weren't meant to stay lost in those patterns. You simply weren't given the chance to understand them.

This is where your real beginning is—not in fixing yourself, but in understanding how you became disconnected in the first place. Once you see how deeply external noise shaped you, you also see that none of it was your fault, and none of it is permanent. Beneath everything you picked up along the way, the part of you that arrived clear is still there, waiting to be heard again.

Welcome to the moment you start hearing it.

CHAPTER 2 – Why You Stopped Hearing It

———

If intuition is something you're born with, if it arrives built-in and effortless, then why does it feel so distant now? Why does something so natural seem unpredictable or hard to recognize? The truth is simple: you didn't lose it. You were conditioned to overlook it.

Children aren't taught to listen inward. They're taught to behave. They're taught to keep the peace. They're taught to avoid upsetting already exhausted adults. The world teaches children that approval is earned through compliance, not connection to themselves. So long before you understood your own inner signals, you were practicing how to mute them.

You weren't taught to ask what feels right to you. You were taught to ask what will keep others comfortable. You weren't guided toward the quiet certainty inside you. You were guided toward the loud expectations around you. Intuition whispers. Adaptation shouts. And adaptation is what you learned first.

When you're young, intuitive signals show up constantly—subtle alerts, nudges, moments of clarity. But the world quickly counters them with familiar lines: don't overreact, don't imagine things, don't be sensitive, stop questioning, calm down, behave, you don't understand yet. The message behind every one of those statements is the same: don't trust yourself, trust us.

That's how the erosion begins.

You learn to ignore discomfort so the room stays calm. You learn to soften what you feel so you won't threaten anyone else's comfort. You learn to overlook clear warnings because someone older insists they mean nothing. You learn to distance yourself from your instincts because adults label them as unreasonable. You learn to turn away from the inner "click" because no one around you recognizes it as something meaningful.

By adulthood, you're fluent in a language your intuition doesn't speak. A language built from people-pleasing, overthinking, shrinking, apologizing, doubting, and accepting situations your body wants to walk away from. It's not that intuition faded. Everything else simply grew louder.

And then life adds survival to the equation.

Survival doesn't care about your clarity or your peace. It cares about repetition, predictability, and minimizing threat. It will always choose the familiar, even when the familiar hurts, because the familiar feels safer than the unknown. Your nervous system isn't trying to sabotage you—it's trying to protect you the only way it knows how.

So each time you sensed something and ignored it, survival celebrated. Each time you quieted yourself to avoid conflict, survival approved. Each time you pretended you were fine, survival rewarded the effort. Every moment you felt that internal click and talked yourself out of it, survival wrapped another layer around your inner knowing.

You didn't stop hearing intuition. You simply learned to obey the noise that covered it.

Then there's belonging—a human instinct so strong it can silence truth in an instant. People will abandon their internal signals long before they risk being left out, criticized, or misunderstood. The urge to stay connected to the group can override clarity without a second thought.

We are wired to remain part of the pack. Intuition is wired to keep us aligned. In the wrong environment, these two forces collide.

When intuition says something feels wrong, belonging urges you to stay agreeable. When intuition notices something is off, fear tells you not to make an issue out of it. When intuition suggests you should leave, unhealthy loyalty insists you stay so you won't lose someone.

So you didn't stop hearing intuition because you failed. You stopped hearing it because every survival instinct in you was trying to keep you safe with the only strategies you had.

And eventually, without warning, the weight of the noise becomes too heavy. The distance between you and yourself becomes too wide. The ache becomes too sharp to ignore. Something inside you taps your attention. That tap isn't intuition coming back. It's you finally turning toward it.

Intuition doesn't disappear. It doesn't weaken. It doesn't age or fade. It doesn't punish you for ignoring it. It simply waits—steady, quiet, patient.

It waits for the moment you get tired of your cycles. It waits for the moment you realize you're repeating what hurts. It waits for the moment you say you can't keep living disconnected. And the moment you reach that point, the channel isn't rebuilt. It's revealed.

Not because intuition returned, but because you finally stopped walking away from where it always was.

CHAPTER 3 – The Problem With Believing What You've Been Told

———

By now you're starting to recognize that much of what you believe about yourself didn't come from you at all. You weren't raised to make choices that supported your well-being; you were trained to mirror whatever dysfunction surrounded you. No one taught you how to work through disappointment, anger, fear, or sadness, so you reached for whatever numbed the ache. No one taught you that genuine happiness comes from being at peace with yourself, from boundaries that protect you, from holding opinions that don't bend at the first sign of pressure. You weren't told that authority can be wrong. You were told to obey it. The world handed you its own confusion, insecurity, and bad decisions, and you were never shown you had permission to choose anything different.

Children don't evaluate their environment with adult logic. They don't look at an overwhelmed parent and think, "They're not handling their emotions well." A child thinks, "This must be what anger or sadness looks like." Kids don't analyze; they absorb. If a child feels neglected or treated like a burden, they don't assume the adult is struggling. They assume they are the problem. They assume they are unimportant, unlovable, unwanted.

Everything they witness becomes a blueprint. They sense when something is off, yet no one shows them another way. Their only model is what they see, and what they see becomes the foundation they build themselves upon, even if they never wanted to resemble it.

Small moments become stories about who they are, and those stories quietly run the show. Most people move through childhood—and, if we're honest, a good portion of adulthood—believing narratives shaped entirely by someone else's pain. You learned through tone, silence, inconsistency, volatility, and adults who had grown bodies but unhealed emotions.

Somewhere in that process, you formed an identity from someone else's limits. Not because you chose to, but because you didn't know you had a choice. Their behavior became your behavior. Their worries became your worries. Their emotional neglect became the belief that your needs were inconvenient. Their unresolved frustrations became the compass you unconsciously followed. Their definitions of who you had to be became the draft of who you believed you were.

No one ever paused to say, "By the way, most of what you're witnessing is not truth — feel free to discard it when you're older." Instead, you inherited their emotional leftovers the same way people inherit old, dented furniture: not because they love it, but because no one mentioned they could let it go.

And then comes the moment — the quiet, startling moment — when you finally realize that the beliefs shaping your life weren't chosen by you at all. They were handed to you through chaos, scarcity, fear, and pain. That recognition is the first spark of your power returning. Because once you see the story wasn't written by you, you understand you're allowed to revise it... rewrite it... or throw the entire thing out and start fresh.

This is where your strength comes back online. Not with fireworks or dramatic epiphanies, but with a steady, "Hold on... this doesn't belong to me" kind of clarity. The moment you question what you inherited, those beliefs begin to lose their grip. You step out of the costume you were shoved into and move toward the person you were always meant to be.

And in that space, you discover something profound:

Nothing was ever wrong with you.

You weren't broken.

You were misled.

CHAPTER 4 – What Intuition Actually Is

———

Intuition is the very first thing you arrived with, and the very first thing the world unintentionally pushed you away from. Before you had language, rules, fear, or explanations, you had an immediate sense of knowing. You didn't analyze — you recognized. You didn't negotiate with yourself — you responded. You didn't talk yourself into clarity — you simply felt what was true and moved toward it. You came equipped with an internal compass, a built-in source of direction that connected you to something wiser than your thoughts. Call it God, call it your higher mind, call it the quiet logic of your biology — the name doesn't matter. The point is that you were created with a way to sense what is right for you. Intuition isn't mystical. It's part of your design.

But because the world teaches you to look outward for answers, many people grow up believing intuition is some rare gift reserved for spiritual experts or people who shop exclusively in metaphysical bookstores. It's not. It belongs to everyone. Every person has that centered, steady internal signal — the one that doesn't shout, doesn't panic, doesn't demand attention. Intuition doesn't try to impress you. It simply shows up.

And it shows up differently than anything else you feel.

Fear is loud and scattered.

Anxiety hums in the background like a faulty electrical wire.

Desire gets theatrical.

Trauma sounds like an alarm.

Overthinking feels like your brain sprinting laps with too much caffeine.

But intuition?

Intuition is a shift — a clean, precise click inside you.

A sudden alignment.

A moment where everything stops spinning and snaps into place.

You can spend hours arguing with yourself, weighing options, spiraling through possibilities — and then suddenly:

Click.

You just know.

And you've experienced that. Everyone has. It's unmistakable.

I once took my dog for a walk because my best friend and I were in conflict and I couldn't stop thinking about it. I kept replaying conversations, imagining outcomes, trying to find the "right way" to fix it. Then, in the middle of all that debris, a single sentence rose up inside me — quiet, clear, and complete:

"What does it matter?"

I froze. At first it made no sense, but then the meaning landed all at once: whether the friendship healed or ended, I would still be okay. The truth wasn't about the outcome. The truth was that I didn't need to fear either path. That realization didn't come from thinking. It didn't come from problem-solving. It wasn't logic. It arrived whole, calm, and undeniable, as if someone handed me the answer without prefacing it.

This is where most people misunderstand intuition. Intuition isn't you thinking. It's something you receive. It doesn't build up gradually or argue its case. It drops in — direct, complete, quiet, certain. You don't generate it. You notice it.

That's why it feels so different from your thoughts. Thoughts spin. Intuition lands.

Intuition can show up as a physical sensation — a tightening, a tingling, a sudden alertness, a subtle jolt, a wave of clarity, a heaviness that says "no," or a lightness that says "yes." It can come as a sentence, a sense, a pull, a pause, or a shift. No matter how it presents, it's directional. It tells you something in a fraction of a second that your mind might take weeks to unpack.

It doesn't ramble.

It doesn't narrate.

It doesn't drag you through your personal history.

It gives you exactly what you need:

A truth.

A direction.

A feeling.

A certainty.

An answer.

And it feels different than your internal chatter — cleaner, wiser, steadier, like the part of you that refuses to let you lie to yourself but will never shame you for what you've done. Intuition is your built-in ally.

Not mystical.

Not dramatic.

Not performative.

Just steady and available.

It has been with you your entire life — observing, nudging, redirecting, waiting — even if you didn't understand what it was. The only reason you stopped recognizing it is because the noise around you became louder. You learned to trust fear. You learned to trust doubt. You learned to trust people who were navigating their own lives with broken internal signals.

Intuition didn't disappear.

You just didn't know what you were listening for.

And when it comes through, your direction shifts almost instantly. You pause. You don't send the message. You take a different route. You stay when you were about to leave, or leave when you thought you would stay. Your body reacts before your logic catches up. You know it's right even if you can't explain why.

Intuition doesn't negotiate.

It doesn't try to persuade you.

It doesn't apologize for being brief.

It simply points.

What you do with that direction is your choice.

You can override it — humans are wonderfully stubborn — but intuition won't punish you for ignoring it. It doesn't withdraw or sulk. It doesn't scold you for choosing chaos over peace. It waits. Patiently. Without urgency. Until you come back tired enough of your own patterns to listen again.

CHAPTER 5 – Choices → Experiences (The Real Version, Not the Motivational Poster)

————

Most people assume their life is a collection of coincidences—luck, timing, circumstance, or some cosmic roulette wheel spinning without pattern. But your life isn't stitched together by randomness. It's shaped. It's patterned. It's directed far more by the beliefs you carry than the choices you think you're consciously making. Your experiences aren't destiny. They're reflections. Not reflections of your worth, but reflections of the beliefs that have been quietly steering you for years.

Every choice rests on something underneath it. Some roots are obvious—you pick the red sweater because you genuinely like red. Some are buried—you stay in a draining relationship because a hidden part of you thinks that is the level of love you're supposed to accept. Some roots were planted long before you had language—you avoid conflict because your nervous system learned to treat disagreement as danger instead of a normal part of human connection.

And here's the thing: the nervous system isn't interested in joy. It's interested in protection. It will choose predictable pain over unfamiliar peace every time, because predictable feels safer, even when it's miserable. If you've ever returned to a situation that hurt you simply because it felt "normal," that wasn't weakness—that was biology doing its best with the programming it had.

This is why people repeat the same stories across different chapters of their life: new jobs, new faces, new relationships, same themes. It's not because they attract negativity or secretly enjoy chaos. It's because the nervous system interprets familiar patterns as safety and unfamiliar patterns as risk. Peace may be part of your design, but discomfort can feel like home until you realize "home" wasn't supposed to feel like tension.

We've been conditioned to view our lives as responses to our environment instead of reflections of our internal world. Most people never question the settings they've adjusted themselves to—they simply stay adjusted. They adapt, endure, normalize, and assume their life is the inevitable result of what's happening around them. But life doesn't mirror the outside. It mirrors the inside.

This is where things become uncomfortable, and also freeing:

most of the experiences that hurt you were not chosen intentionally.

Not consciously.

Not out of self-sabotage.

You chose from what you believed at the time.

And those beliefs weren't born in you—they were inherited.

What you believe shapes everything: what you allow, what you tolerate, what you avoid, what you chase, what you justify, what you settle for, what you refuse, what you think you deserve, and what you let yourself receive. And the experiences that follow don't determine your value; they reveal your beliefs. The good news? Beliefs aren't permanent. They're learned, which means they can be unlearned. And once a belief shifts, your choices shift. When your choices shift, your entire life begins to reshape itself.

It sounds simple, but it's not easy. Changing belief systems means facing the truth that some of the experiences you lived through weren't fate—they were familiarity wearing a mask labeled "normal."

This is why everything begins to change the moment you question the stories you inherited. Self-awareness isn't abstract or mystical—it's neurological. It rewires what your nervous system interprets as safe. Once you understand why you reacted, chose, tolerated, and repeated certain patterns, you're not fixing something broken. You're clearing away the distortion.

Most of us have been living inside a psychological funhouse mirror—one that warped self-worth instead of body shape. And without realizing it, you assumed the distorted reflection was the real you. But those distortions aren't identity. They're learned interpretations you never thought to question.

When you begin to see yourself clearly, you also begin to notice the difference between who you had to be and who you actually are. That clarity doesn't arrive all at once. It comes gradually—choice by choice, moment by moment. Transformation isn't a lightning strike. It's more like sunrise. You don't watch the sun jump over the horizon; you notice the sky getting lighter and only later realize everything looks different.

Your choices work the same way. At first, the shifts are subtle. You pause before agreeing to something that drains you. You catch yourself before apologizing unnecessarily. You feel your body tense around people who take more than they give. You feel warmth around what honors you. You sense peace in decisions that might confuse everyone else. These are signs your internal world is rearranging itself.

And rearranging your internal world is the only thing that ever changes your external one. If you want a different life, you don't begin by rearranging circumstances. You begin by understanding the beliefs that shaped those circumstances. You begin by asking whether you're choosing from clarity or from conditioning. You begin by noticing whether your choices reflect your truth or your fear.

Because when you start choosing from peace instead of pattern, everything begins to shift.

This is the moment your power returns.

Not with fireworks, but with a quiet reclaiming of choice.

You start choosing what supports your life rather than what merely sustains your survival.

And from that point forward, your entire life begins to open.

CHAPTER 6 – The Pain of Disconnection

———

There comes a point in life when something inside you starts to feel slightly misaligned—not in a dramatic collapse, but in a quiet, persistent way. You wake up tired even after sleep. You move through your routines on autopilot. You smile, respond, and function, yet somewhere beneath the surface you sense an internal wobble, a silent question you can't articulate. You don't know what's missing. You just know something is.

Most people mistake this feeling for depression, burnout, or a personal flaw. But it's not weakness. It's not failure. It's something within you stirring, trying to alert you to the fact that a deeper part of you is ready to come online. The disconnection begins subtly—what used to feel meaningful starts to feel hollow. You sense a longing you can't name. It's as though your life no longer matches who you are internally.

You feel restless, yet stuck.

Present, yet not fully alive.

Surrounded, yet strangely alone.

You appear fine on the outside while something in you whispers that a vital piece is missing.

That ache is familiar. I've lived it. There was a time when my life looked functional from the outside, but internally I felt detached, numb, and directionless. I didn't dislike my life—what I disliked was how little I felt like myself within it. I didn't understand who I was anymore, why I was here, or what any of it meant. I felt lost in a way that made me wonder how long I could continue feeling that way.

The difficulty with disconnection is that it creeps in gradually. It's like being lowered into warm water one inch at a time. By the time the temperature becomes unbearable, you've already adjusted. You don't realize something is wrong until the discomfort becomes impossible to ignore.

And then you blame yourself.

You decide you're too sensitive, too emotional, too dramatic, too inconsistent. You assume you're the problem because you can't seem to "just be fine" the way others appear to be.

But here's the truth:

No one is simply "fine."

Some people have just perfected the art of hiding.

If you're feeling lost or unanchored, it isn't because you're incapable of handling life. It's because you were never taught what this feeling actually means. Disconnection is your inner world trying to get your attention, guiding you toward parts of yourself you've never been taught to access. Connection requires information you were never given. So you adapted instead. You observed, copied, and survived.

And survival mode, for all its necessity, is the enemy of inner peace.

Survival is a biological function of your nervous system. It's designed to keep you alive, not fulfilled. It doesn't prioritize happiness; it prioritizes predictability. It's not scanning for joy; it's scanning for the least amount of risk. Pain is familiar, and familiar feels safer than the unknown. So the nervous system will choose predictable discomfort over unpredictable peace, believing it's helping you when it's actually shrinking your life.

But here's what most people never question:

We've been trained to see our lives as reflections of external circumstances—how we were raised, who we were around, what we experienced. Rarely do we ask whether our lives reflect who we truly are, or simply who we became in response to our environment.

That's what disconnection really is:

a life built from reactions instead of choices, from old patterns instead of current truth.

It's like walking through a hall of distorted mirrors. Over time, you stop questioning the warped images. You start believing the stretched, compressed, twisted reflections are accurate. Eventually, the distortion becomes your reality simply because it's familiar.

But the problem isn't you.

It's the mirror.

You've spent years believing you are the product of fear, survival, inherited beliefs, and other people's limitations. You shaped yourself around distortion because no one taught you that the reflection could be wrong. Familiarity became your definition of truth.

But familiarity isn't truth.

It's repetition posing as identity.

The life you're living today isn't a direct expression of who you are. It's a reflection of the beliefs you absorbed without realizing it. And because you didn't know the reflection was warped, you built your life around it—choosing people who fit your wounds, tolerating situations that matched your fear, and repeating patterns that kept the distortion intact.

Not because this is who you are—

but because it's who you learned to be.

Here's the liberating part: mirrors can be changed. Beliefs can be rewired. Patterns can be undone. And when they shift, your choices shift. When your choices shift, your experiences follow. And when your experiences change, your life begins to reflect who you truly are, not who the world conditioned you to be.

It may not be simple, but it is absolutely possible.

And you're already doing it.

Every moment of self-awareness clears a little more of the distortion and brings you closer to your true reflection—steady, grounded, intuitive, whole.

There has never been anything wrong with you.

The mirror was distorted.

And for the first time, you're beginning to see yourself clearly.

CHAPTER 7 – The Moment You Finally Notice

———

There comes a moment when something in your life shifts. It's usually small—so subtle you almost miss it. Maybe it's a wave of calm you haven't felt in years. Maybe it's the sense of being supported even though no one is physically there. Maybe it's a quiet inner phrase that arrives out of nowhere, soft as a breath: "I'm with you." It doesn't announce itself with drama or theatrics. It simply appears, gentle enough that you question whether you imagined it.

And because you've been trained to trust only what you can see, touch, or measure, you brush it aside. But then it happens again. A nudge reminding you where you left something. A whisper telling you to breathe before your mind spirals. A subtle alert correcting your direction before you fall into an old pattern. It begins as a faint shift—almost like the slightest tremble in your internal alignment—because you can feel something inside you that isn't coming from your thinking mind. Something supportive. Something steady.

You start to feel different, as though you're no longer carrying everything alone. Where you once had to force your way through life, adjusting, overriding, and powering through like a one-person survival team, you now sense a quiet companionship. It begins with a moment of clarity arriving exactly when you need it—an insight so simple and so true that it dissolves confusion you've been wrestling with for days. It doesn't shout. It doesn't shame. It doesn't argue. It reveals.

You notice you're not as drained at the end of the day. You notice small moments that soften you, that make you pause, that make you smile. You notice that you're not fighting chaos as often—you're steering. You feel steadier. You feel held. You feel guided.

This is the moment of recognition—the moment you realize there is something within you that is not your anxious mind, not your conditioned fear, not your old survival patterns. And once you recognize it, life feels lighter. The weight you've been carrying loosens, piece by piece.

You sense an internal "I've got you," and you exhale without knowing why. Sometimes the guidance is gentle. Sometimes it's a clear internal stop sign that prevents you from walking straight into trouble. Either way, once you notice this inner presence, you won't lose it again. Not because it suddenly appeared, but because you finally stopped long enough to hear it. You were ready—ready to listen, ready to receive something different, ready to move beyond the life you've been trying to white-knuckle your way through.

This is different from wishing for circumstances to change. Wishing is outward—hoping the world rearranges itself for your comfort. Intuition, awareness, whatever name you give this inner presence, works inward. It gives you clarity, steadiness, and perspective, not possessions or people. It shows you the places where you've been surviving instead of living, functioning instead of choosing, numbing instead of feeling. And that realization stings—not because you failed, but because you recognize how long you've been doing life the hard way when help was quietly available the whole time.

Some people panic when this moment arrives. They worry they're losing their minds, that the voice or feeling is imagined, unrealistic, or dangerous. You can think that. You can push it away. You can return to chaos if you want to. But if you're honest, this is the moment you've been waiting for. This is the moment you unknowingly opened the door to something deeper—not external, but internal—and because you're finally listening rather than overthinking, it can step forward.

And here's the most comforting part: this presence doesn't show up to punish you for losing yourself. It doesn't shame you for the years you felt disconnected. Its purpose is to bring you back. Awareness is the light switch. Once it clicks on, things inside you that felt dark for years become visible again.

Understand this: once you open this inner door, it stays open. Even if you slip back into old patterns, even if you pretend not to hear, even if you distract yourself with noise—you can't un-feel what you've felt. You can delay it, avoid it, deny it, but the awareness remains underneath everything you do. Not because it's demanding, but because it's the truth of you reminding you that you exist beyond your conditioning and above the chaos you once thought was normal.

This is you finally noticing that you were never meant to navigate life alone. You've always had an internal guide—quiet, steady, loyal, present. The world taught you to search outward. This presence brings you inward.

This is the beginning of your return. It's the first crack in the shell you never knew you were living in. It's the hinge moment where you become aware of what has always been there, waiting.

And here's what matters most: this presence does not yell. It does not debate. It does not justify or explain. Every word it gives is truth. It is a navigation system you didn't realize you had, one that was designed to move you toward the life that fits you instead of the life you inherited.

You're waking up to what is yours.

You're not late.

The door didn't close without you.

The moment you arrived was the beginning of the party—

and now that you're here, it's time to begin.

CHAPTER 8 – Hearing It Again

———

When intuition begins to surface again, it doesn't arrive with fanfare. There are no trumpets, no cosmic neon signs, no sudden spiritual fireworks show. It comes the way it always has: quietly, gently, with a familiarity you can't quite place — like a friend stepping back into a room you didn't realize you missed.

You don't force intuition to return. You don't unlock it with enough meditation sessions or manifest it like an overdue package. You don't chant your way into clarity or wait for the universe to drop hints into your inbox. Intuition cannot be summoned on command. It can only be noticed.

And the first sign of noticing is simple:

you pause.

A real pause. The kind that cuts through autopilot. You stop mid-thought, mid-sentence, mid-scroll, mid-surge of emotion. Something subtle shifts beneath your awareness — like someone gently tapping the brakes inside you. You don't know what it is, but you feel it. A quiet internal, Wait... what was that?

That soft interruption is intuition warming back up.

Not loud.

Not intense.

Just present.

Your new awareness clears the static, and the signal becomes easier to recognize.

You begin to feel tiny nudges again.

Small truths.

Quiet realignments.

Thoughts that feel too clean to have been constructed by your mind.

A knowing that arrives without emotional charge.

A pull you can't explain.

At first, you might dismiss these moments. You might assume you're imagining things or overanalyzing. That's normal. Your mind has been running the show for a long time.

But those nudges become familiar.

You start to notice that some thoughts have the frantic tone of your mind — busy, dramatic, overstimulated — and some have a completely different frequency. Calm. Clear. Steady. Unattached.

That's intuition.

Awareness doesn't drop all at once. It arrives in small "clicks."

Like when you're about to say yes out of habit, and a quiet internal no rises before you can think it.

Or when you meet someone and your chest tightens even though your logic says, They seem fine.

That tightening isn't fear — it's information. Your body isn't the source of intuition; it's the speaker system.

Or when you're about to send a message you know is rooted in old patterns, and something inside you steps in with a clear, Not today.

And suddenly... you don't want to send it anymore.

Or when you walk into a room and instantly feel the atmosphere — without a word spoken.

These aren't coincidences.

They aren't flukes.

They aren't silly "gut feelings" that deserve to be ignored.

This is you hearing yourself again.

And it feels different now because you're different now. You're more aware, more honest, more attuned. You've cleared enough noise to finally distinguish between your thoughts and your truth.

Hearing intuition again feels like remembering a language you didn't realize you knew.

You finish insights before your mind starts forming them.

You feel truths that don't need evidence.

You sense red flags before they're visible.

You gravitate toward some people without knowing why.

You drift away from others without guilt or explanation.

And your choices soften, slow, and sharpen in all the right places.

What surprises most people is that the return of intuition often starts in the body — not in mystical visions, but in human sensations:

A warmth when something is right.

A heaviness when something is not.

A pull forward.

A pull back.

A loosening.

A tightening.

A breath you didn't realize you were holding.

A stillness you didn't know you needed.

The body is not intuition.

The body is intuition's amplifier — delivering messages your mind hasn't translated yet.

And now that you're becoming aware, the signals finally make sense. You see them. You respect them. You register them instead of brushing them aside.

Hearing intuition again isn't about becoming supernatural.

It's about becoming available.

Available to your truth.

Available to your clarity.

Available to the part of you that has always known what you needed, long before your mind knew how to process it.

Nothing in your past prepared you for this.

Nothing in your conditioning supported it.

The world didn't teach you how to listen inward.

But awareness — the kind you earned through experience, pain, and growth — opens the channel.

And once you hear intuition again, once you recognize its tone, its timing, its unmistakable clarity, you can't unknow it. You can ignore it if you want. You can delay it. You can negotiate with it. You can overthink it until your mind is short-circuiting.

But you'll still know.

And knowing changes everything.

This chapter marks the turning point — the shift from understanding intuition to experiencing it. From concept to embodiment. From theory to truth.

You're hearing yourself again.

And nothing will be the same.

CHAPTER 9 – Honoring Yourself

———

This is the chapter where intuition becomes action and action becomes self-respect.

There comes a moment — usually right after you begin hearing your intuition again — when you realize something both exhilarating and uncomfortable:

you can't go back to abandoning yourself the way you once did.

You could, technically. Nothing is stopping you.

Free will hasn't gone anywhere.

But something inside you will no longer sit quietly the way it used to.

Ignoring your own truth no longer feels neutral — it feels costly.

Honoring yourself begins with this awareness: every time you turn away from your intuition, you're not just avoiding discomfort. You're trading away a part of yourself. Something real. Something essential.

For most of your life, breaking your own truth became normal.

You didn't call it self-betrayal — you called it:

"I'm being reasonable."

"I'm keeping the peace."

"I don't want to make it worse."

"It's not worth the argument."

"I'll deal with it another time."

"I'm probably overreacting."

"They didn't mean it that way."

"Maybe my expectations are too high."

But here's the reality your growing awareness won't let you avoid anymore:

Every time you abandon your intuition, you abandon yourself.

And the longer you do that, the harder it becomes to trust yourself.

Self-trust doesn't come from confidence.

It doesn't come from motivational speeches in the mirror or pages of affirmations.

Self-trust is built through honoring your signals.

When your intuition says no and you listen — you build trust.

When your intuition says this isn't right and you act on it — you build trust.

When your intuition says you're tired and you rest — you build trust.

When your intuition says leave and you step away — even if your mind panics — you build trust.

When intuition says this isn't who you are and you shift course — you build trust.

Self-trust forms through small choices, quiet actions, and private moments where only you know what you chose.

Honoring yourself isn't grand.

It's not dramatic.

It's not a reinvention montage.

It's steady.

Simple.

Foundational.

The change happens within long before it becomes visible outside.

And here's something people rarely admit:

Honoring yourself doesn't feel heroic in the beginning — it feels inconvenient.

It feels like disappointing people.

It feels like disrupting old patterns.

It feels like making choices that your nervous system, trained for survival, isn't comfortable with.

It feels like saying no when everything in you wants to avoid conflict.

It feels like telling the truth when you were raised to swallow it.

At first, honoring yourself feels like choosing truth over approval.

Choosing peace over belonging.

Choosing intuition over fear.

Choosing alignment over comfort.

It feels backwards because you spent years living forward in the wrong direction.

But something shifts.

Maybe it's the first time you say no and your stomach doesn't drop.

Or the first time you walk away from a situation that used to keep you tethered.

Or the first time you choose rest without guilt.

Or the first time you feel the quiet relief of not betraying yourself.

That relief — that soft, unmistakable exhale — is the first sign of your self-respect returning.

Because self-respect isn't a tone of voice.

It isn't a list of boundaries.

It isn't an attitude or an aesthetic.

Self-respect is the accumulation of choices where you honor yourself again and again until it becomes natural, automatic, effortless.

And here is the truth that changes everything:

Self-betrayal is exhausting.

Self-honoring is sustainable.

Hurting yourself for the comfort of others drains you.

Supporting yourself strengthens you.

Your energy shifts.

Your presence steadies.

Your clarity sharpens.

Your decisions become cleaner.

You're not becoming selfish.

You're becoming aligned.

And beneath that alignment is a deeper truth:

You were never meant to live a life where other people's comfort mattered more than your own clarity.

The world taught you self-abandonment.

Intuition teaches you to return.

Honoring yourself is the bridge between who you were conditioned to be and who you actually are.

And once this truth lands — fully, deeply — you don't feel guilty for taking care of yourself.

You feel responsible for it.

CHAPTER 10 – Choosing Peace Instead of Patterns

———

This is the chapter where your old life stops repeating and your new life begins.

At some point in your becoming, you face a truth most people spend their entire lives avoiding:

you cannot build a peaceful life while choosing from the patterns that once kept you alive.

Patterns are comfortable.

Patterns are familiar.

Patterns are predictable.

Patterns give you the illusion of safety even when they harm you.

Peace is none of those things — at least not at first.

The difference is simple:

Patterns are shaped by fear.

Peace is shaped by truth.

And until now, fear has been making most of your decisions. Not because you're weak, but because you were conditioned to choose stability over authenticity, to avoid loss at any cost, to prevent conflict, to maintain belonging, to stay in the familiar even when the familiar was hurting you. Those choices kept you afloat emotionally, socially, psychologically.

But survival choices do not create peaceful lives.

Survival choices keep the past alive.

Peace choices build the future.

Once you begin honoring yourself, you realize something unnerving: your old patterns try to reclaim command. They slip in quietly, confident in their authority — because for a long time, they had it.

The pattern says:

"Apologize so they don't get upset."

Peace says:

"You didn't do anything wrong."

The pattern says:

"Stay quiet so life doesn't get complicated."

Peace says:

"Truth isn't conflict."

The pattern says:

"Stay — leaving will hurt them."

Peace says:

"Staying is hurting you."

The pattern says:

"Prove your worth."

Peace says:

"You already have worth."

The pattern says:

"You're overreacting."

Peace says:

"You're finally paying attention."

Patterns don't dissolve easily.

They feel ancient because some of them are.

They were built to protect you when you had no other tools.

Patterns are the scar tissue of your emotional life — thick, reactive, and convinced they're keeping you safe.

Peace is the truth underneath the scar.

And the moment you choose peace even once, something inside you shifts in a way you cannot un-feel. Choosing peace doesn't feel triumphant or dramatic — it feels... right. It feels clean. It feels like setting something heavy down after carrying it for too long.

That feeling — the quiet, steady exhale — becomes addictive in the healthiest way.

The hardest part of choosing peace is the first time you do it.

Not because it's difficult, but because it's unfamiliar.

Your nervous system was trained to equate familiar discomfort with safety.

Peace has no data history yet.

It feels suspicious simply because it's new.

But then you choose again.

And again.

And again.

What begins as discomfort becomes neutrality.

Neutrality becomes calm.

Calm becomes clarity.

Clarity becomes confidence.

This is how peace replaces patterns: slowly, steadily, through hundreds of small internal recalibrations no one else sees, but you feel instantly.

Choosing peace doesn't mean withdrawing from responsibility or drifting through life like a spiritually enlightened cloud.

Choosing peace means your choices are no longer powered by fear.

Fear says: "Hurry."

Peace says: "Be honest."

Fear says: "They'll be upset."

Peace says: "You'll be aligned."

Fear says: "If you say no, they'll leave."

Peace says: "If you say yes, you'll leave yourself."

Fear says: "Fix this."

Peace says: "Feel this."

Fear says: "Prove your value."

Peace says: "Show up as you."

And here's the part no one tells you:

When you begin choosing peace, your life stops fitting the version of you that lived in patterns.

Some relationships won't make the transition.

Some habits will fall away.

Some environments will feel too small.

Some dynamics will collapse because they depended on your self-abandonment.

This isn't loss.

This is alignment.

This is your life rearranging itself around the truth you're finally choosing.

You'll know the shift is becoming permanent when choosing peace stops feeling like a rebellion and starts feeling like oxygen.

Your body softens.

Your mind quiets.

Your decisions become simpler.

Your clarity arrives faster.

Your guilt dissolves quicker.

Your boundaries become cleaner.

You stop choosing from panic, obligation, or habit.

You start choosing from alignment.

And when peace becomes your new pattern, something extraordinary happens:

the life you once fought for begins to match the person you're now becoming.

This is the beginning of your stability — not the external kind, but the internal foundation no one can take from you.

CHAPTER 11 – When Peace Becomes Your Normal

───

This is the chapter where calm feels natural, alignment feels obvious, and nothing owns you anymore.

The strangest part of healing isn't the pain.

It isn't the breakthroughs.

It isn't the tears, the clarity, or the sudden urge to overhaul your entire life like you're auditioning for a new identity.

The strangest part — the part no one prepares you for — is when peace stops feeling foreign.

For most of your life, peace was the unfamiliar language.

Chaos was the one you spoke fluently.

Stress was your habitat.

Overthinking was your full-time hobby.

Disappointment was predictable.

Emotional turbulence was routine.

And "fine" was a performance you could deliver on autopilot.

So when peace finally settles in — not as a rare moment but as a state of being — your first reaction is suspicion.

Calm feels like a warning.

Clarity feels like you missed something.

Stillness feels like a trick.

Contentment feels... irresponsible.

Your nervous system whispers,

"Are we sure this is safe? Shouldn't we be bracing for something?"

It's a wild adjustment.

But slowly — beautifully — peace becomes something else.

Not an interruption.

Not a pleasant surprise.

Not the quiet space between storms.

Peace becomes familiar.

And when peace becomes familiar, everything inside you reorganizes.

Your reactions soften.

Your thoughts slow down.

Your muscles unclench.

Your decisions become cleaner and quicker.

Your inner world steadies like a glass of water placed on a stable table after years of shaking hands.

It's not that life stops happening.

Life keeps being life — unpredictable, messy, human.

But you no longer get swept into every current.

Peace isn't the absence of external chaos.

It's the absence of internal chaos.

You stop translating discomfort as danger.

You stop assuming conflict is your fault.

You stop preparing for the worst as a way of protecting yourself.

You stop reading imaginary subtext into neutral situations.

You stop accepting emotional crumbs.

You stop shrinking into shapes that hurt.

Your tolerance for nonsense drops dramatically.

Your patience for disrespect disappears.

Your boundaries become self-evident.

Your self-respect becomes non-negotiable.

You become impossible to manipulate — not because you're rigid, but because you're rooted.

And then the most surprising shift happens:

you stop confusing peace with boredom.

This is enormous.

For people raised in chaos, calm used to feel like emptiness or emotional flatlining.

But now?

Stillness feels like strength.

Slowness feels intentional.

Silence feels clear.

Calm feels safe.

Consistency feels luxurious.

Boredom? It dissolves. What you feel instead is contentment.

You begin craving people who feel like peace, not people who feel like urgency.

You gravitate toward environments that regulate your system, not ones that overstimulate it.

You choose conversations that nourish you, not drain you.

Drama stops being interesting and starts being irritating.

Red flags stop looking intriguing and start looking like the exit sign they always were.

You stop chasing intensity — because you finally understand that intensity was never intimacy.

It was just your nervous system misfiring.

And here's how you know peace has become your new normal:

Your reactions change before your circumstances do.

The situation that once shattered you?

Now it barely creates a ripple.

The comment that once ruined your week?

Now it slides off.

The behavior you once tolerated?

Your entire body says, Absolutely not.

The guilt that used to follow your boundaries?

Gone.

This isn't numbness.

It isn't indifference.

It isn't detachment.

This is regulation.

This is alignment.

This is awareness.

This is inner leadership.

Peace becomes your baseline, not your peak.

And with that shift comes a new kind of confidence — not loud, not performative, not brittle, but quiet and grounded. You don't know everything, but you know yourself. And that is enough.

When peace is your normal, you don't react to life — you respond.

You don't fear uncertainty — you navigate it.

You don't brace for impact — you trust your footing.

You don't apologize for your clarity — you follow it.

The world hasn't gotten easier.

You have become steadier.

And now — with this steadiness anchoring you — you're finally ready to let intuition guide your direction instead of just your awareness.

CHAPTER 12 – Trusting Your North Star

———

This is the chapter where knowing becomes direction and your life quietly changes course.

Once peace becomes your normal, something remarkable begins to unfold: intuition stops acting like an occasional insight and starts functioning like a steady guide. Not mystical. Not theatrical. Not "ask the universe for signs and hope it replies." Real guidance — calm, consistent, familiar.

It shows up as small confirmations.

Soft inner nods.

Quiet agreements between you and yourself.

You'll be in the middle of a thought, a task, a moment — and feel a gentle inner "yes." It's so subtle you might miss it, yet so distinct it stands apart from everything else. Or you'll feel a clean "no" — not fear, not hesitation, not anxiety. Just a clear, effortless that's not it.

This is your North Star.

Not a star above you — a star within you.

A knowing that doesn't demand attention but offers direction.

Most people never experience this because they never learn to trust themselves. But once peace settles into your life, intuition feels like a language you suddenly remember how to speak.

It feels natural.

It feels obvious.

It feels like returning to something ancient inside you.

You begin to know things without explaining how.

You sense direction without analyzing options.

You feel truth long before any evidence arrives.

You can't justify it to others — and you no longer try.

Because intuition doesn't argue, and neither does truth.

People may not understand your choices, but that's because your choices no longer come from the outside world. They come from the deeper place inside you that no longer negotiates with fear, guilt, or obligation. A place that simply knows.

And once you start trusting that knowing, small synchronicities begin appearing like breadcrumbs:

You think of someone — they reach out.

You leave early — and avoid something you didn't realize was coming.

You say no — and something better arrives in the space that opens.

You walk away — and clarity meets you immediately.

You rest — and inspiration drops in unannounced.

You follow a nudge — and end up exactly where you need to be.

These aren't coincidences.

They're alignment in motion.

For years, your choices were rooted in survival — repetition, memory, fear, old stories. Now your choices begin to align with intuition — and intuition aligns with truth. That's why life starts feeling smoother. Not perfect, but less forced.

You're no longer pushing your life.

You're following it.

And with each small act of following, your fear of the unknown begins to dissolve. Not because nothing scares you, but because you're no longer navigating blindly. Your navigation is internal now.

The outside world used to be your map.

Now it's simply the landscape.

The map lives within you.

And that changes everything.

The more you trust your intuition, the less you depend on external validation or approval. It's not that you stop caring about people — you simply stop outsourcing your clarity.

You don't ask for permission.

You don't wait for agreement.

You don't water down your truth to make it easier for others to digest.

You don't poll the room before moving.

You don't need reassurance to act.

You feel the click — and you move.

This doesn't make life flawless.

It makes you capable of navigating life with steadiness.

Intuition doesn't erase uncertainty.

It erases confusion.

Because confusion is never a lack of clarity — it's fear clouding the clarity you already have. Once you begin trusting your North Star, confusion becomes a rare visitor. You may feel uncertain — that's human — but you will not feel lost.

Being lost comes from being disconnected from yourself.

You are no longer disconnected.

Trusting your North Star makes your life quietly steady.

Your movements shift.

Your voice softens yet strengthens.

Your choices carry intention.

Your presence becomes grounded.

Your boundaries become effortless.

Your direction becomes clear.

People may not fully understand you — but they'll feel the difference. Something inside you settles. Something inside you strengthens. Something inside you knows.

You are no longer easy to wobble.

No longer easy to sway.

No longer easy to shape into who others want you to be.

You no longer abandon yourself to belong.

You no longer debate what you already know.

Your North Star becomes your compass.

Your peace becomes your anchor.

Your intuition becomes your navigation.

And from here, your life transforms because it finally aligns with the truth of who you are.

The next chapter prepares you for the world — because the world will still be loud, but you won't be shaken by it.

CHAPTER 13 – The World Will Still Be Chaotic (But You Won't Be)

———

There's a truth no one tells you when you begin healing, reconnecting, and trusting yourself again:

the world does not change with you.

People don't suddenly develop emotional intelligence.

Life doesn't turn into a serene meditation retreat.

Your inbox doesn't become polite.

Traffic doesn't vanish.

Your family doesn't download new personalities overnight.

Strangers still behave like wildcards.

And the general population still treats self-awareness like an optional course they definitely skipped.

The world keeps being the world — loud, messy, unpredictable, often resembling a circus where the toddlers seized control.

But you?

You stop matching it.

This is one of the most disorienting — and liberating — shifts you'll ever experience. For the first time in your life, your internal state no longer depends on the noise, moods, or chaos of the people around you.

You become emotionally sovereign.

Not hardened.

Not detached.

Not numb.

Not cold.

Just sovereign.

Meaning:

You choose what enters your inner world.

You choose what influences you.

You choose what you absorb.

You choose what you release.

You choose how far external chaos travels inside your internal space.

You begin living with a quiet kind of resilience that doesn't require effort.

It isn't forced composure.

It isn't pretending.

It isn't "being the bigger person."

It's simply what happens when you're no longer disconnected from yourself.

When you're rooted in peace, chaos can't uproot you.

You notice it.

You adjust to it.

You respond to it.

But you don't lose yourself inside it.

Someone else's tone no longer hijacks your stability.

Someone else's panic no longer becomes your crisis.

Someone else's insecurity no longer determines your choices.

Someone else's anger no longer makes you question yourself.

Someone else's expectations no longer outrank your intuition.

You begin responding instead of reacting.

Observing instead of absorbing.

Pausing instead of spiraling.

Choosing instead of defaulting.

This is where emotional adulthood finally settles into place.

You stop personalizing other people's behavior — because you clearly see their behavior is about their inner world, not yours.

You stop rushing to fix everything — because other people's discomfort is no longer your emergency.

You stop carrying emotions that don't belong to you — because they feel immediately foreign.

You stop trying to manage everyone else's peace — because you've finally found your own.

When peace becomes your baseline, you stop "catching" other people's chaos.

You can sit inside a storm without becoming the storm.

You become the calm within it.

Not because you're enlightened.

Not because you're trying to prove something.

Not because you're rising above anyone.

But because your inner world is no longer up for negotiation.

This makes boundaries natural — not harsh, not defensive, just clear.

A boundary from peace simply says:

"I don't need to push you away.

I just need to stay with myself."

And then something surprising happens:

you begin seeing everything more clearly.

Not cynically.

Not judgmentally.

Not through hardened eyes.

Just clearly.

You see patterns without absorbing them.

You see dynamics without being confused by them.

You see manipulation without feeling guilty for noticing it.

You see red flags without painting them green.

You see what's yours — and what is unquestionably not.

And the best part?

You stop taking things personally that were never personal.

Someone's bad day doesn't become your emotional spiral.

Someone's insecurity doesn't become your responsibility.

Someone's expectations don't become your obligations.

Someone's chaos doesn't become your assignment.

You stop sacrificing yourself to save people who aren't asking to be saved.

You stop shrinking to earn love.

You stop abandoning your truth in the name of keeping the peace.

Here's the power of inner peace:

you can be in the world without becoming of the world.

Suddenly that phrase doesn't sound lofty or spiritual — it sounds practical.

You can love people without losing yourself.

You can support people without carrying their storms.

You can empathize without absorbing.

You can stay centered while the world around you shakes.

Your life no longer depends on external stability — which means your stability no longer collapses every time your environment shifts.

This chapter marks the transition from internal clarity to external mastery.

And now — with your peace anchored, your intuition active, and your sovereignty forming — you're ready for the next step:

Living a life guided from the inside out.

Which brings us to the next chapter — one of the most potent, distilled truths of the entire book.

CHAPTER 14 – The Quick-Grab Wisdom Section

———

Truths to reach for when you forget who you are.

These aren't quotes.

They aren't affirmations.

They're reminders — the kind that bring you back into alignment the moment life pulls you off-center.

They land quickly.

They settle deeply.

They recalibrate instantly.

Take what speaks to you.

Carry what stays.

Return to what restores you.

———

PEACE & CLARITY

Peace isn't something you achieve — it's something you uncover.

You don't search for calm; you uncover what was buried beneath the noise.

Peace isn't a prize — it's your natural setting.

Stillness isn't dull — it's your nervous system finally exhaling.

Chaos shouts because it doubts itself; peace stays quiet because it doesn't.

If something weighs you down, it's not aligned. If it feels light, it is.

INTUITION

Fear makes noise; intuition delivers truth.

If you created it with your mind, it's thinking. If it arrived on its own, it's knowing.

Intuition never debates — it simply appears.

Truth doesn't compete for your attention; it lands and stands.

If it spirals, it's your mind. If it clicks, it's intuition.

Intuition whispers because truth doesn't require volume.

You can exist in the world without becoming tangled in it — intuition is how.

SELF-WORTH & IDENTITY

You were never "too much" — some people were simply too limited.

You're not overly emotional — you're perceptive.

You weren't damaged — you were misled.

Your worth never fluctuates, no matter who fails to recognize it.

You don't need approval to be yourself.

Self-respect begins the moment you stop abandoning your own truth.

BOUNDARIES & ENERGY

A boundary isn't a barricade — it's clarity about how connection can happen.

If you feel drained around someone, that's information.

Protecting your energy is a responsibility, not a flaw.

You owe no one access to the version of you that no longer exists.

Those who benefited from your silence may accuse your boundaries of being "attitude."

HEALING & GROWTH

You're not beginning again — you're continuing with awareness.

You didn't waste years — you gathered understanding.

Growth initially feels like loss because old versions of you can't come forward.

Healing isn't becoming whole — it's realizing you always were.

Awareness isn't pain — it's expansion stretching into place.

Your patterns weren't failures — they were protection.

CHOOSING YOURSELF

Honoring yourself is quiet; abandoning yourself is chaotic.

Every "no" to misalignment is a "yes" to your own clarity.

You're not difficult to love — you simply refuse partial affection now.

Your future self is already steady; you're just stepping into their life.

Truth doesn't need defending — only living.

You do not have to diminish yourself to soothe someone else.

———————————

LIFE & DIRECTION

Peace isn't something you manifest — it's what remains when the noise is removed.

Clarity doesn't raise its voice — it settles into place.

You arrive the moment you become aware.

Anything that costs your peace is overpriced.

Uncertainty isn't a threat — it's space for possibility.

The life you want grows from the choices you were once too exhausted to make — until now.

———————————

KEEP THESE CLOSE.

Write them where you'll see them.

Carry them in your mind, your pocket, your heart.

These truths aren't motivation — they are recalibration points.

Each one is a compass placing you back in your own direction.

CHAPTER 15 – Becoming Who You Were Meant to Be

———

This is the moment you stop searching for yourself — because you finally meet the version of you that was there all along.

Becoming isn't about adding layers or building a new personality.

It isn't reinvention.

It isn't remodeling.

It isn't self-improvement in the surface sense.

Becoming is remembering.

Remembering the self you drifted away from.

Remembering the self you quieted to survive.

Remembering the self you reshaped to be acceptable.

Remembering the self the world never taught you to trust.

For most of your life, the message was the same: be more of this, less of that.

More agreeable.

Less reactive.

More logical.

Less sensitive.

More patient.

Less visible.

More "easier to handle."

Less you.

But the truth is simple:

You were never too much — you were unsupported.

Becoming who you were meant to be isn't about striving; it's about releasing.

Releasing the conditioning that told you your needs were excessive.

Releasing the guilt that grew out of other people's fears.

Releasing the beliefs you absorbed but never chose.

Releasing the patterns designed for survival, not peace.

Releasing the distorted mirrors that shaped how you saw yourself.

You aren't becoming better.

You are becoming true.

And when that realization lands — fully, unmistakably — your life begins to shift into a form that feels almost uncannily right. Not flawless. Just aligned.

Becoming looks like this:

Choosing without fear.

Speaking without apology.

Resting without self-judgment.

Loving without shrinking.

Walking away without collapsing.

Staying without abandoning yourself.

Protecting your peace without asking for permission.

Following your intuition without negotiating with it.

You stop chasing lives that were never meant for you.

You stop performing for people who never noticed the effort.

You stop trying to earn love from those unable to offer it.

You stop mistaking chaos for depth.

You stop treating crumbs like connection.

You begin living from your center instead of your wounds.

And as you do, something extraordinary happens:

Life stops resisting you and begins meeting you where you are.

The right people feel grounding.

The right opportunities feel easeful.

The right environments feel supportive.

The right choices feel clear.

The right pace feels humane.

The right path feels unmistakably yours.

This is the life that waited for you.

You simply couldn't see it while you were in survival mode.

And just as important as what enters your life is what naturally falls away.

When you become who you were meant to be, you no longer cling to anything misaligned.

You no longer negotiate your value.

You no longer beg for reciprocity.

You no longer accept emotional scraps.

You no longer carry what isn't yours.

You no longer confuse familiarity with truth.

You stop pouring your energy into places that cannot hold it.

Because becoming isn't fragile — it's powerful.

It's soft, but unyielding.

It's kind, but self-honoring.

It's loving, but never self-erasing.

Becoming is the end of pretending.

The end of performing.

The end of explaining.

The end of shrinking.

You stop returning to places that hurt you once you understand they never matched who you are.

You stop holding on to people you've outgrown.

You stop repeating patterns that were never meant to be permanent.

You stop censoring your truth to make your existence easier for others.

You begin walking in your fullness — the version of you that existed long before the world convinced you to dim your light.

And here's the most important part:

Your future self — the grounded, peaceful, intuitive, steady version of you — isn't waiting on perfection.

It's waiting on recognition.

That version of you has been here the entire time — beneath the fear, behind the conditioning, beneath the noise.

Becoming who you were meant to be is the final return.

A return to your peace.

A return to your clarity.

A return to your intuition.

A return to your truth.

A return to yourself.

You're not becoming someone new.

You are becoming who you really are.

And the world — the aligned world, the one meant for you — opens the moment you do.

CHAPTER 16 – Your Becoming Is Already Underway

I f you've reached this point in the journey, it means something inside you has already begun to shift. You may not feel transformed. You may not feel enlightened. You may not feel like you've "arrived." But you have arrived in the only place that matters: awareness.

Awareness is the doorway.

Awareness is the turning point.

Awareness is the first step of every becoming.

Nothing changes in your inner world until you can see yourself clearly — and the moment you do, everything begins to unfold differently. Not dramatically. Not instantly. But steadily. Quietly. Naturally.

Here is the truth beneath every struggle, every doubt, every moment you thought you were failing: you were never broken. You were never lost. You were never behind. You were simply disconnected from the part of you that always knew the way.

And now, without forcing it, without performing it, without even fully understanding how it's happening, you are reconnecting.

Piece by piece.

Click by click.

Choice by choice.

Moment by moment.

You become more yourself each time you listen to what feels true.

You become more yourself each time you choose peace over the old pattern.

You become more yourself each time you honor what your intuition gives you.

You become more yourself each time you stay with yourself instead of abandoning yourself.

You become more yourself each time you set down the weight that was never yours.

This journey isn't linear.

It isn't polished.

It isn't perfect.

But it is real.

And it is yours.

And it is already happening.

You do not have to rush the process.

You do not have to force clarity.

You do not have to earn peace.

You do not have to prove your worth.

Everything you have been seeking outside yourself — clarity, belonging, steadiness, direction — has always lived within you. Your intuition is not a new arrival. Your peace is not a new skill. Your alignment is not something you build from scratch. They are not new creations — they are original parts of you that you are finally returning to.

And you are returning.

You are learning to hear yourself again.

You are learning to honor yourself again.

You are learning to trust yourself again.

You are learning to stand with yourself again.

You are learning to live as yourself again.

Becoming isn't a future event.

It is a present movement.

It shows up in the way you pause before reacting.

In the way you notice what feels wrong instead of dismissing it.

In the way you choose differently — even once.

In the way you forgive yourself a little faster.

In the way you speak to yourself more gently.

In the way you protect your peace with more ease.

In the way you stay standing when chaos arrives instead of collapsing under it.

You are not waiting to become.

You are becoming.

You are not at the start of your journey.

You are already on the path.

And here is the truth that matters most as you move forward: peace is your compass. Intuition is your guide. And you — the real you — are the journey.

Not the past.

Not the pain.

Not the patterns you've outgrown.

Not the roles you were handed.

Not the stories you inherited.

Not the beliefs you carried for years.

You.

The one underneath the noise.

The one who is finally being heard.

The one you are finally returning to.

Walk forward with that.

Choose from that.

Trust from that.

Live from that.

Your becoming isn't ahead of you.

It's already in motion.

And it's only getting brighter from here.

Also by Kelly Logan

365 Days of Truth Volume 1
365 Days of Truth Volume 2
365 Days of Truth Volume 3
Sense to Soul How To Have A Personal Relationship With God
Through Mystical Interpretation of Scripture
The Cause And Effect Survival Guide
Intuition: The Best Friend You Didn't Know You Had

Watch for more at www.betterbyintent.com.

About the Author

Kelly A. Logan is an author and creator who teaches intentional living through cause and effect, not hype or motivation. Her work focuses on decision-making, intuition as biological awareness, and building stability through practical choices. She is the creator of the *Better by Intent* framework.

Read more at www.betterbyintent.com.

www.ingramcontent.com/pod-product-compliance
Lightning Source LLC
Chambersburg PA
CBHW071110090426
42737CB00013B/2551